T0413418

NOTRE DAME
FIGHTING IRISH

BY CAMERON CLENDENING

The Child's World®
childsworld.com

Published by The Child's World®
1980 Lookout Drive • Mankato, MN 56003-1705
800-599-READ • www.childsworld.com

Copyright ©2022 by The Child's World®
All rights reserved. No part of this book may be
reproduced or utilized in any form or by any means
without written permission from the publisher.

Cover: Robin Alam/Icon Sportswire/AP Photo.
Interior: AP Photo: John Swart 11; John Mersits/
Cal Works Media 15; Tony Tomsic 16; Joe
Raymond 19. Library of Congress: 8 top. Newscom:
Stephen M. Dowell/TNS 20. Shutterstock:
Photo Works 12. Wikimedia: 7, 8 bottom.

ISBN 9781503850361 (Reinforced Library Binding)
ISBN 9781503850620 (Portable Document Format)
ISBN 9781503851382 (Online Multi-user eBook)
LCCN: 2021930282

Printed in the United States of America

*Touchdown! Time
for the Fighting
Irish to celebrate.*

CONTENTS

WHY WE LOVE COLLEGE FOOTBALL

The season is turning to Fall. Excited crowds fill stadiums. Pennants wave. And here come the fight songs. It's time for college football! The sport is one of America's most popular. Millions of fans follow their favorite teams. They wear school colors and hope for big wins.

Notre Dame is one of college football's most famous teams. The school has had many famous players, coaches, and games. They are known as the Fighting Irish. They have won 11 national championships. There is nothing quite like a fall afternoon in Notre Dame Stadium!

It's another packed house at Notre Dame Stadium for Fighting Irish football.

CHAPTER ONE

Early Days

Notre Dame has been playing football since 1887. They lost their first game to Michigan, 8-0. They did not beat the Wolverines until 1909. After that, Michigan refused to play Notre Dame until 1942!

Notre Dame's first big win came in 1913. The Irish **upset** national powerhouse Army at West Point.

The Fighting Irish had some other good seasons back then. From 1915 through 1917, they lost only three games. Football at the school changed forever in 1918. That's when Knute Rockne became the coach.

WHY FIGHTING IRISH?

Notre Dame is a **Catholic** school in South Bend, Indiana. The football team was first called the Catholics. Newspapers nicknamed them the Fighting Irish. Many Irish people are Catholic. Today, fans often just call the team the "Irish."

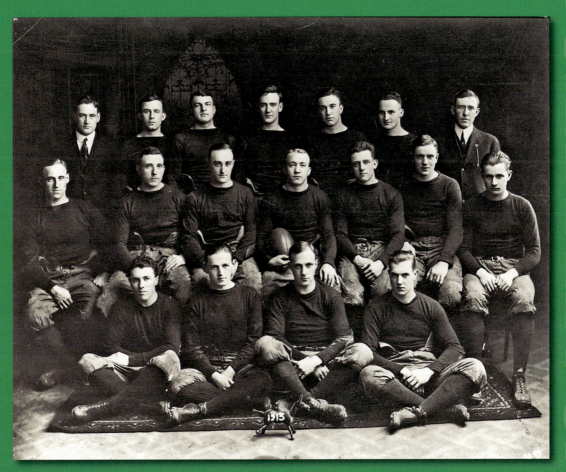

This 1913 Notre Dame team upset Army 35–13.

NOTRE DAME
FIGHTING
IRISH

Left: Knute Rockne became a national legend as Notre Dame's coach.

Below: Rockne (far left) posed with his 1925 Fighting Irish team.

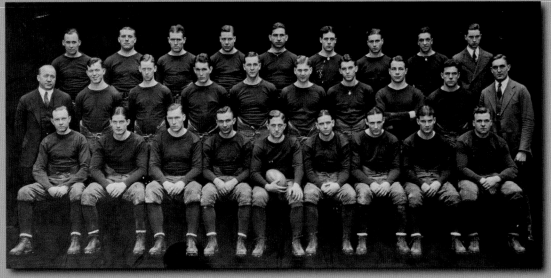

CHAPTER TWO

Glory Years

Coach Rockne made Notre Dame truly great. He led them to national titles in 1924, 1929, and 1930. He was a tough leader. He became so famous, a movie was made about his life.

That was not the end of Notre Dame's winning. They won four national titles under coach Frank Leahy. Those came in 1943, 1946, 1947, and 1949.

The Irish were not done! They were national champs in 1966 and 1973 as well.

In recent years, the Fighting Irish have come close to winning three national titles. They played in the 2012 national championship game. In 2018 and 2020, they reached the College Football Playoff. Notre Dame fans always believe their team will win it all!

CHAPTER THREE

Best Year Ever!

Few schools have had as many great years as Notre Dame. Their 1988 team might have had the hardest road to the top.

That year, quarterback Tony Rice led the way. Coach Lou Holtz was in charge. Notre Dame played a tough schedule. They beat four teams that ended up in the top 10! Their biggest win came in the last regular-season game. They traveled to play number-two ranked USC. The Irish forced four **turnovers**. They beat the Trojans 27–10.

The Fighting Irish faced West Virginia in the Fiesta Bowl. Notre Dame's 34–21 win made them national champions!

Right: Running back Tony Brooks rumbled over a West Virginia defender in the Fiesta Bowl. ►

Notre Dame Traditions

No college football team has more traditions than Notre Dame!

The team's golden helmets are famous. They look like the Golden Dome that tops a building on campus. Before every game, the helmets get a clean coat of gold paint.

Notre Dame's locker room has a famous sign. It reads "Play Like a Champion Today." The players tap the sign for luck.

Notre Dame's **fight song** is a college classic. It is called the "Notre Dame Victory March." It was once voted the greatest fight song of all time!

THE BIG RIVAL!

Notre Dame first played USC in 1926. Many fans consider this college football's greatest rivalry. It has produced more national championships and Heisman Trophies than any other matchup!

◄ *Left: Former linebacker Manti Te'o shows off the famous golden helmet.*

CHAPTER FIVE

Meet the Mascot

Notre Dame's mascot is the **leprechaun** (LEP-rih-kahn). That is a tiny, lucky character from Irish folklore. A Notre Dame student dresses as the mascot. He leads cheers at games. He also gets fans excited at a big **rally** before home games.

The mascot is also in the school's logo. It **includes** a leprechaun with his fists raised!

NOTRE DAME STADIUM

The Fighting Irish play in Notre Dame Stadium. The stadium opened in 1930. Knute Rockne led the Irish to a national title that season. Sadly, he died in a plane crash in early 1931. The stadium is nicknamed "The House that Rockne Built."

Right: In 2019, Samuel Jackson became the second African American Notre Dame student to perform as the famous leprechaun. ➤

14

Joe Montana

CHAPTER SIX

Top Notre Dame QBs

In 1943, quarterback Angelo Bertelli won Notre Dame's first Heisman Trophy. The award goes to college football's best player. QB Johnny Lujack won the award in 1947.

Joe Theismann played for the Fighting Irish from 1967 to 70. Theismann had a great season in 1970. He finished second in the Heisman Trophy voting that year.

JOE COOL

Joe Montana is one of the greatest QBs of all time. He led the Irish to a national championship in 1977. Then, he joined the San Francisco 49ers of the NFL. He became the first QB to win four Super Bowls. Montana was nicknamed "Joe Cool." He was always calm in the toughest games.

Other Notre Dame Heroes

Notre Dame is not just about Heisman winners. **Defensive tackle** Alan Page helped win the 1966 national title. He was an NFL star, too. After football, he became a Minnesota **Supreme Court** judge!

Ross Browner played defensive end from 1973 to 1977. His fierce tackling helped win two national titles.

Raghib "Rocket" Ismail was a special player. He was a wide receiver and kick returner. He used speed and quick moves to score touchdowns. "Rocket" finished second in the 1990 Heisman voting.

> ### THE GIPPER
>
> Running back George Gipp was Notre Dame's first member of the All-America team in 1920. Sadly, he got very sick. He wanted his teammates to remember him. Before he died, he asked Rockne to "win just one for the Gipper." That story was in a 1940 movie, "Knute Rockne, All American."

Right: Former player Alan Page later came back to speak to Notre Dame students. ➤

CHAPTER EIGHT

Recent Superstars

The list of great Notre Dame players continues. In 2012, **linebacker** Manti Te'o finished second in the Heisman Trophy voting. That is a very rare feat for a defensive player.

In 2017, offensive linemen Quenton Nelson and Mike McGlinchey were both All-Americas. Both were also picked early in the NFL Draft.

Ian Book started at quarterback for the Irish from 2018 to 2020. In 2020, he led them to the College Football Playoff. Book was the QB for 30 wins in his career. That's the most by any QB in Notre Dame history.

Who will be the next star to add to Notre Dame's great history?

◄ Left: In four years, Ian Book threw 72 touchdown passes. He also ran for 17 scores.

GLOSSARY

Catholic (KATH-uh-lik) a Christian religion followed by more than one billion people around the world

defensive tackle (deh-FENSS-iv TAK-ul) a football position at the center of the line of scrimmage

fight song (FYTE SONG) a tune played to rally sports fans

leprechaun (LEP-rih-kahn) a tiny, lucky character from Irish folk stories

linebacker (LYNE-bak-er) a defensive position that plays behind the line of scrimmage

logo (LOH-goh) a design of letters or numbers that stands for a school

rally (RAL-ee) a gathering of college sports fans before a game

Supreme Court (soo-PREEM KORT) the highest level of court in a state or country

turnovers (TURN-oh-vurz) plays on which an offensive team loses the ball to the defense

upset (UP-set) beating a team you were expected to lose to

FIND OUT MORE

IN THE LIBRARY

Jacobs, Greg. *The Everything Kids' Football Book*. New York, NY: Adams Media, 2018.

Sports Illustrated for Kids. *The Greatest Football Teams of All Time*. New York, NY: Sports Illustrated Kids, 2018.

Steele, Michael R. *Miracle Moments in Notre Dame Fighting Irish Football History: Best Plays, Games, and Records*. New York, NY: Sports Publishing, 2018.

Temple, Ramey. *Notre Dame Fighting Irish*. New York, NY: Weigl, 2020.

Wargin, Kathy-jo. *Win One for the Gipper: America's Football Hero*. Chelsea, MI: Sleeping Bear Press, 2004.

ON THE WEB

Visit our website for links about the
Notre Dame Fighting Irish:
childsworld.com/links

Note to Parents, Teachers, and Librarians: We routinely verify our Web links to make sure they are safe and active sites. So encourage your readers to check them out!

INDEX

ABOUT THE AUTHOR

Cameron Clendening has written football books about USC and Notre Dame. A native of Dallas, Cameron is an accomplished football player himself, having earned co-Offensive MVP honors as a wide receiver during his senior year of high school.